Patterns

Poems by Constance Patrick

Praise for Poetry by Constance Patrick

Constance's natural gift is her mastery of images. She paints images in her poetry that are so vivid the reader is left with powerful pictures. And these pictures elicit feelings that often run quite deep. Reading her poems become emotional experiences.
– Janie Rian, Retired Therapist/Social Worker, Writer.

Constance writes with wit and candor. She is a brilliant wordsmith, enticing the reader with detailed description, inviting you into her world. Tender stories as well as fantastic lunacy weave their way into you, until you are filled up, nourished, and whole. Reading these poems will be a delightful and satisfying experience.
– Martha Entin, Poet and Playwright, Sedona, AZ

Patterns, *Constance Patrick's collection of poetry, looks to the sky, touches our soul and compels us to search our hearts The fluid phrases awaken the spirit and invite us to question and explore the patterns of our lives and the world around us. Her poetic verses linger in the mind long after the pages are turned as we beg for more.*
– Carole Nese, Creative Non-Fiction Writer and Poet, Los Angeles, CA

Constance's poetry begs the reader to explore deep into the universe, deep into culture and deep into self. It is a journey of discovery and occasionally laughter.
– Mary Scully-Whitaker, Corrections Consultant/Photographer, Marine on St. Croix, MN

Constance Patrick's poems are a snapshot of human emotions and life experiences that provoke thought and leave an imprint. Each poem is masterful in its ability to create a scene for the reader to journey through and relate to their own life. Constance's depth of knowledge of each poetic form she uses, shows a genuine love and respect for her craft with every word.
– Nicole Kroll, Operations Manager and Consultant, Lafayette, LA

I really enjoy reading Constance's Poetry and Short Stories. She seems to pick a theme or subject, then shares it with her readers in a very thoughtful, interesting way. I think you will have a very good read with this book, enjoy!
– Jacque Patrick, Master Docent Phoenix Art Museum, Glendale, AZ

Expressive and articulate, Constance Patrick uses the English language to paint a picture the same way an artist would use their brush. Her creative spirit flows through the words of her script.
– Molly Busby, Internal Support at Maximus, Phoenix, Az

Constance brings a unique eye to any situation or place, with kindness, clarity of detail, and often a sly sense of humor.
– Kate Hawkes, Red Earth Theatre Producing Artistic Director, Poet & Writer, Sedona, AZ

Constance speaks from real life experience and is a master of forms leading her to a unique ability to creatively draw the reader into a vividly portrayed moment. She has been an inspiration to me from the beginning of my poetry writing, her encouragement and direction has led me into the writing of poetry and I can easily say that I've found my voice because of her ability to gracefully teach and support.
– Nancy Ruby, Artist and Poet, Sedona, AZ

Constance Patrick is a former teacher, entrepreneur, performance actor and author. Her craft includes short stories, screenplays, one-act plays, and monologues. A published poet, her new book of poetry is a continuation of her lifelong passion for writing, and a desire to use her craft to make a difference.
– Bruce Patrick, IFMA Facilities Manager, Six Sigma Black Belt

Fortunately for us, there are poets like Constance Patrick who fearlessly open their hearts for us all to see, and in so doing we feel our hearts opened too. This is where the courage in writing lies, and putting words to paper that ring this true requires an immense amount of it.
– Paul Longstaffe, Founder of Western Edge Writers, Los Angeles, CA

Copyright © 2022 Constance Patrick, Sedona, Arizona

All rights reserved. No part of this book may be reproduced in any form or by any electronic or mechanical means, including information storage and retrieval systems, without permission in writing from the author.

ISBN-13: 979-8-9871202-0-0

Cover photo: IStock

Book design: Naomi C. Rose

Text set in: Times New Roman

Word Crafter Press

WordCrafterPress.com

Dedication

To my parents: for their love and unwavering support as my interests in life grew beyond a teaching career.

And to the "green book" — it opened the windows of creativity for me, exposing me to styles of poetry I had never learned about at University. So thank you Wauneta Hackleman, editor of The Study and Writing of Poetry: American Women Poets Discuss their Craft *(1983)*

Table of Contents

About Poetry...viii

Perspectives
Heroes...2
I Am Called...4
Incarnations...6
Pausing...8
Stars...9
Shadow Walking...10
Thinking Outside the Box...12
Uncharted...14
What's Next?...15

Remembrances
Could It Be the Wine?...18
Friend...20
Libby...21
Gypsy...22
May 24, 2022...24
On the Night of Diwali...26
Sweet Summers...28
The Bandit Queen...30
The Train from Lake Como...32

Truth Be Told
Before the Masked Ball...36
Belonging...37
Creativity...38
If Walls Could Talk...40
My America...42

Sons and Daughters...44
T. K....46
The Collective...48
Thirst...50
Who Do We Forgive...52
Midterms...54

Love or Not
Dear Johnny, I'm
  Available...56
You...59
Just Another Believer...60
Knowing You...61
Lover...62
Once Upon a Disney
  Knight...63
Pretty Words...64
Thanks to the Moon...66
The Rune...67
When the Stars Rise Up...68

Does it Resonate
i know this...72
Inside the Empty...74
it's just me...76
The Ant in Shakespeare's
  Tempest...77
Journey...78
Solstice Yearnings...80

Placeholders...82
Star-falls...84
Whisper Mode...86
What Is This Burden
   We Carry?...88

Grateful

4 x 7 lines of me...92
Brought Forth...94
Floating...96
On Forgiveness...97
Prayer of Peace...98
Grace...99
I listen to my heart...100
Meditation...102
Rituals...104
Sometimes...106
Soul...107

Nature

Breaking Dawn...110
Cypress in Moonlight...112
Fire Light...113
Patterns...114
Simply Bold...115
Winter Sky...116
Starry Night...118

The Sea...120
Outside...22

Just for Fun

1648...126
OT...127
El Rey and
   The Homonyms...128
Holiday Pie...130
Socks...132
Wobble-bobble...133
The Singing Platoon...134
Free Range...136
Those Dickens Kids...139

Acknowledgments...140
About the Poet...142

About Poetry

Poetry can be charismatically brief as in a Haiku of 17 syllables, or an epic story of love and friendship, fate and free will, and honor as in Homer's The Iliad. Poetry's message can charm. Irritate. Become an anthem. Recall history. Sit in reverence to Mother Nature, or in judgment of her. Create a story worthy of song lyrics. Or reveal secrets and innuendos on many levels with many layers.

Poetry is the bait on the hook. And whatever its intent, poetry hooks us into the perspectives of life events. It helps us see the depth of love. Feel the anger of current events, or feel aligned with them. Smell the fresh mown summer grass, or the metallic smoke from a recent bomb's residue. We hear a hummingbird's wings, and equally the loud cheers when a whale is released from an ice flow. We can taste the fresh peach pie at Grandma's house, and the four different lasagnas at a reception after shedding tears at the cemetery.

But we also depend on poetry to bring us closer to lesser-known senses: the vestibular, and the proprioception. These other two sensory experiences (the 6th and 7th) are connected to the tactile sense, or touch. But neither is anywhere close to the sense of touching sandpaper, silk, or gooey syrup. The vestibular sense involves movement and balance, and how, or if, we are moving.

Proprioception is about one's body or position interacting with one's surroundings: the walls closing in on us, a speeding car screeching to a stop five feet from us, the feel of cold damp fog wrapping around us, clumsy or stick figure stepping in soft sand, pushing or pulling, or falling through an abyss.

Yet poetry also engages us in an eighth sense: interoception. Feeling hunger, suffocation, dry mouth, pounding heart, a migraine coming, the onset of depression, etc., all relate to the sensations of the body. Interoception refers to the body's physical condition and what the body's organs are feeling.

And poetry can wrap up all the above in numerous styles, such as Etheree, Lune, Nonet, Tango, Rondeau, Villanelle, Quintain, Free Verse, Septet, Interlocking Rhyme, Clerihew, Triolet, Lanterne, The Manardina, Onda Mel, etc. Poetry can rhyme or not rhyme, be in stanzas or not, and can require the writer to create lines with one syllable or hendecasyllabic (11 syllables per line), decasyllabic (10 syllables), heptasyllabic (7 syllables), etc.

Poetry encompasses everything we experience. The length? Unimportant. The form? Unimportant, but enticing. Its perspectives about life? Revealing.

I have come to believe over and over again that what is most important to me must be spoken, made verbal and shared, even at the risk of having it bruised or misunderstood.
–Audre Lorde

Perspectives

Heroes

Heroes – teachers of time

rescuing or destroying all in their path

in the name of someone's Truth.

Heroes – burst onto killing fields,

protecting the old, infirm, the vulnerable,

seeking all the lost children –

in the name of someone's Truth.

The best of heroes-all seek another village,

fortress or fiefdom to raze or spare,

or seek new terrain for another tyrant,

their unwavering duty disseminating *someone's* Truth.

The best of heroes-all rise to the top, saviors of others,

or stoop to measure havoc and chaos on others' souls.

But these blood-stained heroes finally come

to the shoreline of their own truth,

staring at the sunset or sunrise wondering

"How have I magnified all the good?"

The best of heroes-all go to the shoreline of their hearts,

wash themselves free of evil deeds and bloody rescues,

offering their penitent hearts

to a forgiving god for blessings, protection, endurance,

for sharper swords, more destructive bullets and explosives.

Sunrise…brings beauty, renewal, hope, faith,

new gifts and new evils to exact on the world.

Sunset…offers solace, safety, places to rest and

withdraw from the demands of *doing* in careless, unruly times.

Heroes-all endure, tired from living someone else's truth.

So I let my heroes of old drop their causes, their spears,

their swords of death and destruction,

their shields of protection.

I look along an empty horizon

now asking *"Where are my heroes?"*

My heroes stand beside me,

stand with me every day

breathing beauty, kindness, love and compassion

into the world, into the ether,

breathing with the heart of the divine holding us safe.

Arriving at the shoreline of my own truth,

I am wondering *"Have I magnified the good…even once?"*

I Am Called

I am destined –
called this day
to kill the bull.

Through a tiny slit in the wall,
a confused weakened foe smells me,
raises its heavy head. Our eyes meet.

Starved, tranquilized,
bloated from high-salt feed,
it refuses weakness.

A challenge snorts from the dark cell.
I straighten, tall and proud,
puffing up my assurance beyond its challenge.

I feel its danger.
It smells my vulnerability.
We know each other.

"I am royalty in the ring", I say softly.

"I survive *all* goring threats."

Silence. The bull knows itself.

Wanting to charge, it paws the crushed rock.

Still its weakened alpha dares me –

demands I bow.

Eye to eye, we hold our truths firm.

I turn away from its willful endurance,

praying I don't die today.

Larry Kane

Incarnations

messengers in flow

and messages

1's, zero's, dots, dashes, blanks

constructed, deconstructed, delivered

from flowing synchronicity

filling

immense incomplete interludes

of ourselves out of sync

messengers

and messages

cutting us from our cipher spaces

shaping our blanks into wholeness

filling

our unknown that is nothing

with something –

loving-kindness, perhaps

messengers

and messages

calling us up, down, to, from,

work done or beginning

and more work to do

oiling the molecular chains and pulleys

of time and purpose

with compassion, perhaps

messengers

and messages

unending

Pausing

eastern wind weaves

through desert acacias –

fragrance

from golden button-balls

threads through life

scented wind drifts

willfully wedging itself

between

the dysfunctions of the day

hoping to unlock a moment

on the other side of time

where troubled souls pause

feeling

spring lift them all

above the edge of chaos

Stars

When stars stick to the opaqueness of night

we wonder why the sky won't let them fall.

Singing *Twinkle, twinkle little star* feels so trite,

but we love how stars stick to the night,

and love a loose shooting star, or fast satellite.

Yet deep within we need to know, driven to recall,

if we're divinely birthed from that black opaque night

or did heaven open a back door and just let us fall.

Shadow Walking

hop scotch, chalky faces, hit or miss games
jumping rope in timed rhythm-waves
campfires, badges for safety and sewing,
all the silly Scout-girls I didn't look like
and Kool-Aid filling the gaps

boys destroying anthills and grasshoppers
sun through glass orbs delivering their slow death
boys giggling, beating their chests, yelling
they dominate the unknown. I disconnect
waiting for a soothing glass of Kool-Aid

daily reminders I carry original sin
I'll never be good enough for God
I'm damned! so pray! be good all day
and maybe I won't go to hell
oh, how I sucked down the Kool-Aid

now, reliving old tapes and story boards,

the cocoon of self wants the wings of butterflies

to fly to the other side where accumulation of pain

lights the path to new portals, new memories

and no one offers even a taste of Kool-Aid

I want to walk through pain-points,

through the veil between lies and truth,

beyond the semantics of justification

beyond disregard, dismissal, indifference

I choose to walk beyond the edge of my shadows

Thinking Outside the Box

Oh how we love our Crayola color collection –

152 possibilities – a box with an endless selection.

My dog has the colors *Sepia, Sienna*, and *Tumbleweed*.

And a dab of Desert Sand can highlight a reed or a seed.

Seasonal haystacks can be orangey Mac and Cheese.

Asparagus, Olive, and Inch Worm color leaves and trees –

this box of possibilities and choices unending

calls my imagination to flights of color-bending.

Boxes hold 24, 48, 96 and one hundred twenty,

but my colors are missing from every box of plenty.

Enough of *Tumbleweed, Sand, Mac and Cheese*.

Did they forget to name one *The Bees Knees*?

The names do not name the moments of me,

the *Silent Sound of Harmony*,

or on my breath, *Peace Dancing*,

nor any moments wild and enchanting.

What colors do I recommend to Crayola?

Not gladiola, pensacola, or gorgonzola.

They need *Thunder Mountain* or *Dove in the Rain*,

Monarch Orange or *Ley Line Terrain*.

Perhaps *Javelina Gray, Hazel-Green Creek,*

or quail's *Scurry* and *Squeak*.

Do they not have *Sumac Red* or *Sycamore Gold*,

or the color *Fallen Tree with Histories Old*?

Please, Crayola, conjure a color for *Love Heals Us*.

And a color for *The Sanctity of Trust*.

Don't give me another color of insignificance.

Give me the color of *Sacred Silence*,

the color of *Loving Kindness*,

and *Forgiving is Timeless*…

a crayon for *Love and Compassion*,

another for *Positivity in Action*.

And if they can make them that refreshing and new,

then I can be grateful for the color called: *I Honor You*.

Uncharted

Is it bad times I travel in
or just a bad time to travel?
An irrelevant question perhaps.
My journey at times seems
laid out, specific, predictable.
Then the curve ball slides in –
my journey takes a turn,
at times unsteppable,
unmanageable, unstoppable.

It's a familiar journey –
I feel it, know its demands.
Smooth or rough road
hasn't changed where I land.
Come hell or high water
this journey is mine.
I'm set for good times and bad
keeping my soul's compass in hand
for the uneven, unsteppable times.

What's Next?

from chaos comes need

need for patience of mind

mind must stop, be still

still enough for a prayer

prayer for safety, pray

pray for harmony, pray

pray for mutual respect

respect a prayer sending love

love the feeling of calm

calm bringing focus

focus on lies dressed up as truth

truth must be true in our hearts

hearts holding the compass of kindness

kindness leading to hope

hope is what's next…

next to hope lies a dream.

dream of peace.

Memories and thoughts age, just as people do. But certain thoughts can never age, and certain memories can never fade.
– Haruki Murakami

Remembrances

Could It Be the Wine?

In Tuscany

a ten by ten

rock-squared space,

with ancient dusty

cracked tile floor,

supports my poetic dreams

of deftly uttered words

freed from my mind

flowing on paper

and dancing through the air

or could it be the wine

floating my colorful words

so loud,

sailing them

over aging vines,

old lives and older times

even if no one heard them

my mind would still create

a place like this

in Tuscany

for lovers

destroyers

renewers

poetry and wine

Friend

Your

"hello"

embraces –

gathers me in,

keeps me from falling

into deeper grayness,

lifts me from heavy shadows

chasing old memories tethered

to pain hiding in my empty eyes.

Your "hello" helps me find my breath and smile.

Libby

I met her once

a tiny significant moment

of delicate smiles

and graceful conversation

it was not meant to be

that I would know her

in the on-going moments

of our lives

only that I was to follow –

as sand follows the wave

back to the ocean

Gypsy

gypsy

hiding behind her soul

clapping hands a fast

pap-pap, pap-pap-pap

tapping strapped heels

clack-clack clack-clack

red hot skirt billowing

flashy fabric snapping

earrings glittering long

back arched

arms curved

hands flying

fingers dancing

hips flicking,

soul's rawness

filling her breasts,

gestures broadening

muscles flaring

body exploding

in waves

in dance

in escape

in passion –

innuendo

invitation

in waves

undulating

May 24, 2022

Games often end in ties –
    second chances and tie breakers
    played out
    proclaim one winner.
Home team and adversary know,
in a stand-off,
sudden death yields a victor.

May 24 allowed no overtime,
    no extra innings or walk offs,
    no "last-ups" to see whose last breath
    could sustain a win.
That day offered no option for a draw, for
extra rounds, or more time to play –
no breath or scream affected the outcome.

There was no time to run, or chase
    the adversary away for a victory.
    There was no contest, no match,
    no margin for a win.

Time was up at game's end –

in a heartbeat's standoff

no tie, no tie breaker.

The 21 hosts, overwhelmed,

    lay in streams of blood –

        visitor scored an insurmountable lead then

        perished at the end of his own game.

On that day in Uvalde

no second chances, no winners –

only sudden death.

On the Night of Diwali

(Festival of Lights)

Your life circled the drain in endless rhyme,

drugs a quick fix, but your demons wouldn't tame.

How long you drug-played was a matter of time.

You found solace in highs sold by alley slime,

drawn by their dull light, moth to the flame.

Your life circled the drain in endless rhyme.

The devil had his own sneaky little paradigm

shifting your opposing realities into deep shame.

How long you drug-played was a matter of time.

Your hope for a better world was a pantomime

asking forgiveness from the parents you blamed.

Your life circled the drain in endless rhyme.

For decades they sacrificed to help you climb

beyond heroin, opioids, meth, cocaine.

Your life circled the drain in endless rhyme.

You took the devil's gift he called *prime* –

that one lethal overdose ended your game.

Your life circled the drain in endless rhyme.

How long you drug-played was a matter of time.

(Note: Diwali, festival of lights, symbolizes the spiritual "victory of light over darkness, good over evil, and knowledge over ignorance.")

Sweet Summers

I loved summers with Grandpa,

his breakfast routine a fond memory:

crisp crunchy bacon,

eggs over easy and super runny,

scorched coffee percolated with egg shells –

and nothing more than a few coffee grounds –

toast burnt blacker than coal…

the charred layer carefully scraped off,

and fresh sliced peaches

bathed in heavy cream.

Best memory of all though

he'd hold my hand on our weekly walk

down Glengyle to Delta Ave. –

Kroger's homemade peach ice cream

tempting our tastebuds with each step.

It never melted on the walk home,

just waited to rest at its honorable place

in the small freezer, front and center

after a scoop for Grandpa and one for me.

Fidgety and wiggly, I could hardly wait

to find those tiny chunks of peaches

secretly hiding in the sweet, creamy,

extra smooth peach ice cream.

We counted our tiny bits of peaches –

whoever had more got a kiss on the cheek.

Grandpa always let me win.

The Bandit Queen

Belle Starr rode wild over dry deserted land
craftier than snakes slithering on sand.
Belle Starr, survivor, living off her lies –
black dress, plumed hat, dark calculating eyes.

Theft, stealing horses, and prostitution –
wicked ways shaping Belle's evolution.
In her band of rustlers, thieves and felons,
Belle was well known as the maven of guns.

She had outlaw Cole Younger with her glance
then found other villains for her romance,
living with Sam Starr, a Cherokee guy,
then took up with a Creek named Jim July.

One day angry shots rang out fair and square.
Belle jerked then buckled above her black mare.
The slayer shot Belle in the neck and back,
her head snapped, tossing off her hat so black.

She fell from her horse, blood running bright red.

Shot two, into the face, and Belle was dead.

Many were blamed but never found guilty –

thus, her killer remains a mystery.

Locals and dime novels are not on par

for who shot the evil thieving Belle Starr.

Too many untruths run rampant and mean

for this legend known as the *Bandit Queen*.

The Train from Lake Como

Running late

for Lake Como-Zurich train.

The chug and wheeze surged

as I pulled onto the boarding steps.

Our hands touched.

I tingled with energy.

Threading through

a tunnel of bodies

we reached as one for the window,

chuckling at our intense need to breathe.

Crisp misty air swirled in,

deep inhaling made us laugh.

We poked our heads out

catching wispy chilling vapors

dropping from the Alps.

Tossing her head upwards,

hair whirling, dancing fiercely,

her unimprisoned laughter

wrapped alpine moments around us.

Leaning back, resting on me,

she trusted my presence,

my essence, my energy.

Our ears warmed against each other's,

our breath escaped drifting as one,

my skin tingling again.

She turned – our eyes smiled

with an easy comfort and gratitude.

Zurich, a magical feast

of laughter, joy, love,

and goodbyes –

until next time

on the train from Lake Como.

Even a happy life cannot be without a measure of darkness, and the word happy would lose its meaning if it were not balanced by sadness. It is far better take things as they come along with patience and equanimity.
– Carl Jung

Truth Be Told

Before the Masked Ball

Mirror, Mirror hung in the hall

I am not short nor am I tall,

I am not big, and I'm not small.

Your mean view's just a catcall

planned to catch me in a sad pall.

My feet let me walk, past a crawl,

my fingers write beyond a scrawl.

Mirror, Mirror through me you trawl

looking for faults to make me wrawl

with sounds louder than a cat's brawl.

Mirror, Mirror you have such gall

thinking you see me, know it all.

Lies cry out from your wailing wall.

If I believe your vile cabal,

down a rabbit hole I will fall.

Belonging

keys belong in locks

opening doors and secrets

peaches waiting in baskets

inviting summer delights

goldfish in bowls

finding no way out

coffee in cups

holding the wake-up call

savings belong in hiding places

loose change in pockets and jars

clouds belong in the sky

releasing rain for the earth

sunrise belongs to the horizon

bringing a new day

a flame belongs to the wick

but its light belongs to everyone

Creativity

Sometimes

it's as easy as boiling water

and little dried leaves creating tea

Sometimes

it's the brilliance

of morning's fire in the sky

painting a new skyscape

Perhaps

it's the tumble of dogs and cats clouding up into elephants

taking on a blast of pastels or red-hot peppers

Perhaps

it's staring at the conjoined trees separate and free

only above their heart chakra,

tossing about, releasing random joy

Maybe

a leaf hopper or lizard re-charging

unseen solar packs

or

an unending stream of tiny ants untouched

by religion, politics, angers and hates

Maybe

it's about butterflies, the lilt of their dance on a breeze

or soft landing on a tiny flower

or

fireflies

writing unknown lyrics on the night sky

Sometimes

it's the same gaseous points of light

or a full moon sailing

the depth of night's ocean

Sometimes

it's nothing – no words, thoughts, images –

just me stuck in the immovable creative void

And then

I call on the one

who dwells on the tongue of poets

and the window of words opens

If Walls Could Talk

I feel

bombs exploding,

shaking and breaking ancient structural bodies,

bricks and mortar cracking and crumbling

near my own storied walls.

I wait –

patience thin, fear mounting

with each deadly bombardment

closer.

I stare

at Grandfather's hand carved mantle

above the blackened hearth,

and winter seeping from it

scaring away the desire for flickering light

or the laughter it once kindled.

It's rockets now that flare and burn.

I cherish

the old body of clay on the mantle –

Grandmother's rugged caring hands

pulled a lump of clay into a soft round shape,

a vessel for seeds, for Spring, for rebirth.

Generations of hands fed the round clay body –

no scratches or cracks marred its simple beauty,

its purpose for abundant futures intact.

I wait.

Memories flood me –

a kaleidoscope of smiles and celebrations

around the seed pot, the round clay body of birth.

Shellfire screams by,

detonating outside my broken window.

The body of hope topples.

I watch

its graceful descent.

The rumbling cascade of bombs

mere yards away does not move me.

I feel

the seeds in my pockets, and know

we'll go into the ground together

to grow again.

My America

rolling fields, urban hubs

summer splashings, hydrants and creeks

winter despairs and darkness ignored

gutters run full with trash

liquids, solids, and

unmistakable stench

yet sidewalks, stairwells, and parking lots

hold space for the empty souls

behind empty eyes

the big fix is just big talk –

discourse flushes into disintegration

disintegration mirrors aged patterns

patterns shape outcomes!

did my vote change that?

did my vote bring about change?

will disintegration lead to discourse?

will patterns of disregard

ignore the gutters, always?

will we forgive our own walk-bys?

will the chalice of freedom

continue quenching our thirst

or overflow with darkness?

will the hateful ever feel grateful

the disenfranchised, whole and safe,

those struggling, become equal?

will America still covertly or overtly

anchor new dreams draped over old ones

so my America becomes

the beacon of hope again?

Sons and Daughters

We run from terror still, and brutal atrocities,

as our ancestors ran from czars and ruling squatters.

We say goodbyes until phones have dead batteries,

and fill trains with scientists, musicians, and authors.

We save our mothers, children and babies –

the vulnerable sent away with grandfathers.

We hold the front line against adversaries

who believe old lies wrapped in new fodders.

We are Ukraine.

We are her sons and daughters.

The invaders, they too leave their homes and families

for easy wins in deep white drifts of frozen waters.

Ignorant of their ruler's thirst for commodities,

they melt in their tanks, becoming human solder.

We shut down all of our kind reciprocities
when Russian troops advance as marauders
bombing our homes, churches, and cities –
for they believe their top-ranking defrauders.

We are Ukraine.
We are her sons and daughters.

These aggressors trust their leader's mythologies –
and sacrificing their lives will never feel odder
than drowning in their own blood and animosities
face down, eyes forever open, on a field of slaughter.

Russia thrives on empty promises and false apologies.
So we are steadfast against these dull minded plodders –
they will never control our hearts, land or communities.
We are freedom fighters: here, now, reaching broader.

We are Ukraine.
We are her sons and daughters.
Unconquerable.

T. K.

Theo – five foot six,

forty-two, pale, slightly pudgy,

wispy-thin hair with a mind of its own

belying his tales of once thick

golden angel's hair.

A former monk still deeply spiritual.

A generous smile framed big imperfect teeth,

the front two spaced apart, each a bit sideways.

Wired from the git-go,

he never needed caffeine,

life was a jolt all by itself.

A scattered silly man

sitting on his grease-spotted tie everyday

to press it,

yet never flat enough,

and never in contrast to

overly wrinkled clothes

snatched from a corner pile

in a room he rented

from some vague someone no one knew.

Theo's small bright eyes saw it all.

His outrageous uncensored humor shot out

as a speeding bullet from his mind to his mouth,

a masquerade harboring untold truths.

Theo – everybody's friend, brother –

guarded unnamed secrets behind his eyes

in a very deep place where he held

a lost soul

searching for itself.

The Collective

we, from nowhere, settling everywhere
cellular composites in a tight cocoon
dangling in a meaningless time-space snare
until birth and blood rights are karmically hewn.

we, ready to rejourney through an unsettling
version of ourselves; we, waiting to be unraveled
without judging or critiquing, without meddling,
as if every star-path of every journey traveled

counts how many times we failed or died
how many times refreshed, renewed, rejected –
deciphered, decoded, or denied –
composites cast off? or cherished, protected?

how many uncountable times dangling, waiting –
wrapped up so tight in karmic repetition
good and evil always asking, debating
is this, our birthing time, our last iteration?

waiting, resolutely, as time-space passengers

recalling deeds and regrets forgone,

reborn as siblings of destiny, tiny messengers

with the mettle and courage to carry on.

in time, a thousand layers fall away

we are exposed, no more clever packaging

sins, angers, hates reveal us, betray

our bare selves barely managing

and when the wind blows right,

the collective soul that binds us

detaches; we drift then take flight –

released again as seeds of kindness

Thirst

Hard packed soil

disconnected,

divided from itself.

Fissures, cracks

waiting for rain.

Brittle twigs and thirsty vines hosting

crisp tongues of foliage

hanging on

divining space…

waiting

for drops of a random drizzle.

Ungrounded,

my strength, beliefs –

brittle, and charred

by the brutal heat of

anger, lies and manipulation –

overflow with impatience, doubt.

I'm desperately divining space,

pushing through these fractured moments,

reaching

for random drops of ...

I'm waiting

for a refresh

of truth and hope

in a drop of rain

and how it tastes on my tongue.

Who Do We Forgive

Do we forgive the killers of others? Those

born without a script or playbook on how

to be whole, be a friend, engage, rebuff hate,

stand strong in a bully's weak shadow.

Who forgives the killers of self?

They are their own avatar lost in life's

video game, stuck on replay and multi-play,

their souls breaking apart.

Can we forgive the "golden badges" taught to profile,

exerting too much restraint, shooting before asking,

shooting…as they're trained to,

because they fear for their own lives.

Do we forgive ourselves for judging the killers,

the communities that hold them, the imperfect systems,

the parents that abuse or abandon them, and all the

bullies degrading them, labeling them less than.

Can we forgive humanity for teaching us to hate,

to minimize others, distrust others, perpetuate

the overriding belief others are less than ourselves,

others are insignificant.

When do we forgive the victims for being

in the right place-wrong time, waiting

for the hard hand of deliverance

to take them home, and us to a painful abyss.

And when do we forgive ourselves,

for demanding change, yet expressing

no gratitude for not being chosen

to be a victim, or a catalyst for change.

Midterms

Politics! Muck and mire displayed!

Candidates' poison darts –

seeking rivals – cut deep with lies and blame.

Respect falls to charade.

Falsehoods, from looms of lies, spin a

shame game.

Love or Not

Never love anyone who treats you like you're ordinary.
– Oscar Wilde

Dear Johnny, I'm Available

My deepest secret I ever kept
was my crazy love for Johnny Depp
until the bar mirror held my steady look
as Mr. Tall and Handsome stared, and I shook.
He surveyed the bar then sauntered right in
all confidence riding in on a sin.
Shirt, shorts, tan to a sunny bleached blond
my heart fluttered, racing out to bond.

His lazy swagger and easy glide
caught a weakness my eyes couldn't hide.
He took up the stool right next to mine
my heart skipping a beat out of line.
Bright eyes with a smile and a wink –
was I drunk on only one drink?

Oh how my heart fluttered, stirred and turned over
finding he smelled of honey and sweet clover.
And he owned me.

I fell for kisses from his sky-blue eyes,

his kisses in moonlight hiding his lies.

We had the right words and big happy hearts,

a pair made in heaven or unknown parts.

We were together as one and the same,

we agreed then I had to have his name.

Oh how my heart fluttered, stirred and turned over

knowing he smelled of honey and sweet clover.

And he owned me.

He swaggered into a room so time would stop, lock,

everyone's eyes turned in dead silence sans tick-tock.

When my friends snickered and said her name…

we were no longer one and the same.

Rumors said he had a new girl,

tongues wagged he gave them *all* a whirl.

I thought of Johnny Depp and started a letter.

Dear Johnny, I wrote, already feeling better.

Still my heart flutters, stirs and turns over

knowing he smelled of honey and sweet clover.

He still owned me.

Hundred dollar bills fell behind his curse,

none falling into my barren coin purse.

Every week my paycheck partied with his boys

and dwindled faster on his newer big boy toys.

He trashed my pretty clothes and fancy makeup,

didn't want to risk, he said, a nasty breakup.

I lingered long in my sweet daydreams

creating forever-new love themes.

I shrank, wasted away to unpretty and teeny

while he bought silk ties and a fast red Lamborghini.

He always looked dashing, and suave

with tailored suits and shirts so mauve.

I wanted to feel a lot better

so again started on my letter.

Still my heart flutters, stirs and quickly turns over

recalling that smell of honey and sweet clover.

He had owned me.

Now my heart flutters, stirs and turns over –

I killed him. It's finally over.

I felt better and started my letter.

Dear Johnny…

You

rose petals

in peach

drift lazily

languidly

to the ground floor

of my mind.

gathering there,

perfumed layers

spark a reminiscent

glow of warm love.

tones of amber-orange

gold and autumn

smile up

at the drifting petals

that spell your name

pattern your face,

texture your love

color your friendship

petal soft

glowing

lasting

warm

Just Another Believer

I call the fog,

wrapping up my heart, *Love* –

music, dancing, flowers

and promises feel like love.

I released caution

for the dream of love –

a new moon night, shooting stars,

words dripping with sugar,

the quarry holding

our naked bodies up to heaven.

Daylight,

burning off the fog

and the dream,

exposes this rocky ledge.

I find myself alone

in the quarry

wondering if I'll hold

a quarry-baby in nine months

like the other believers

caught in the fog.

Knowing You

cinnamon
    amber
    magenta
mint
    violet
    chartreuse
clove
    azure
    russet
nutmeg, thyme
    scarlet-crimson-senna
    sun-butter-lemon-flowers
knowing you
my mind drinks in
spiced rainbow gardens

Lover

i see you

i do

and will

    tomorrow

maybe

i want you

i do

and will

    tomorrow

maybe

i love you

i do

and will

    tomorrow

let me

Once Upon a Disney Knight

You,

the shining knight

on the glorious white steed

You, riding into my life

saving me from me,

from angst over my life

You,

mastered me,

dominated, berated.

You

are

poison.

Pretty Words

i look to the stars and beyond
into black holes holding audience
with untouchable galaxies
the void in me mirrored in midnight

you come near, sit softly,
settle into the sky with me
slightly touching my awareness
volumes of dark voids
cast me off into the now
into you, into us

your face defined by moonlight
your fingers slightly traveling me
arm mine tingles
skin mine sighs
your eyes…your eyes –
sweet, caring, softer than air
messaging your soul to me

with pretty gentle unspoken words

kindness wrapping every atom of you

into every moment of me

caught, captured, captivated

helpless, hopeless –

falling endlessly into your soul-space

my unyielding heart folds over

melting into your love

Thanks to the Moon

love is here

in the moon shadows

but I wait.

moon caresses me –

i drift, i sway,

i slow into slow

into shadows of slow.

my heart cries into the moon.

music gathers me

moves and dances me.

moonlight cascades

on a face in the shadows

a face reigning in passion,

desperate puppy eyes

begging me

to pause, look, invite,

begging for release –

heart-eyes wide open begging me

to see, feel, embrace.

i invite.

The Rune

Love lost is a heart bleeding on a blue moon.

Moon, and the woeful heart, cry tears from within.

Within this moment and moments past,

past reveals patterns repeating –

repeating behaviors I have not let go.

Go, I say, grasp a message from a rune –

rune tells *All hearts fall to the blue side of the moon.*

When the Stars Rise Up

When you loved me, the stars kissed the sky,

their brilliance sticking on the blackness of night.

Wrapped in your love I drifted up into a new freedom –

from a scar-hardened heart I rose up for your touch.

Your litany of *forever words* branded my heart –

I couldn't see when you brushed me away, didn't know

I was just vapor dispelled in a boundless black night

until I felt your disdain searing my heart and soul.

I am expendable, a castoff from your comet's tail.

Fear and loathing hold me in a void nuanced

with subtexts of the almost said should have said

would have said could have said – but didn't.

When the stars rise up to kiss the midnight sky

I remember us in a sliver of moonlight

holding each other steady, the way stars

clutch the sky to keep from falling into nothingness.

We touched the primal sky so easily, only to find

we were lovers and friends who would be enemies.

Heart in hand, I must learn to see in the dark again,

and hope an angel catches me as I'm drifting by.

Lots of people want to ride with you in the limo, but what you want is someone who will take the bus with you when the limo breaks down.

– Oprah Winfrey

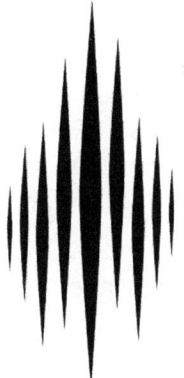

Does it Resonate

i know this

ink, scribed, stains paper –

messages linger, waiting

as if more is to come.

I breathe

as if

I know the message.

birds, bees, butterflies

lift and lilt in unseen dimensions

as if dancing on melodies of nectar.

I breathe

as if

I know the nectar.

snowflakes

melt in place on earth's face

as if they know to stay.

I breathe

as if

I know this stay-place.

unseen messages linger

melodies of snow melt in place

dimensions of breath lift and lilt

I breathe

because

I know the nectar.

Inside the Empty

How brazen, the sky night so dark,
to let the cadence of shooting stars
fall heavily on my hearing –
fall like little taps on a hundred snare drums.

How insolent, the sky night dark,
to show off the abundant trails of
star-glitter fanned out like wakes of water
behind a meandering boat
exposing the magic of its own dark self.

How generously sky night dark shares its
panther black skin with fiery star points
holding the fabric of night in place,
until the hands of the clock pull
the curtain of darkness to a lower horizon
and the empty of darkness, dragging itself along,
leaves a residue in the absence of
breathing, seeing, being.

Will my dark and light push and pull,

give and take…share enough space

to honor each other and each one's purpose?

Or is purpose also in absence?

How impudent the day sky bright

to let the cadence of sunbeams soldier in

through eons of time and distance

with daybreak's brilliant message

falling into the I shadows of me.

it's just me

my habits and quirks belong to me

and maybe one small idiosyncrasy

I fill space with time and time with space

and hope I have kept kindness in place

at times being human is fraught with rigors

challenging as chess and hostile as chiggers

I belong to this tribe, whether right or wrong,

and I don't want risk being un-belong.

The Ant in Shakespeare's Tempest

He wanders haltingly over the lettered page,

working his way to the top

in circular unplanned transport

weaving through spaces

moving between lines,

hesitant, undecided,

swaying on classic words.

I am absorbed, journeying with him.

Stop start change. Stop start change.

He breaches over the top margin,

to a thin paper's edge,

balances,

drops off.

While he wandered

I wondered

if he got anything out of it.

Journey

I was ready to go, and going –

eyes closed I could feel myself drifting, then

sailing with light year speed though nothing

and everything.

Speeding through sheer interstellar clouds,

a low hum –

a familiar rumbling vibration –

filled me with sweet energy, as if

returning to Source.

I slipped further away into nothingness,

no entrance, no exit, no harbor

no stars or star shadows

only recognizable sounds

floating me

into thick blurry walls of water,

holding me suspended in a kind,

telling baritone cadence

It is not your time, go back –

do more good.

Eyes still closed,

I felt water surrounding me. Blinked.

And again.

Staring at opaque black air above,

I sensed an unending end of myself –

no weight, no finite edges of me

in an endless extension of eternity –

embryonic oneness in a float tank.

Solstice Yearnings

Alone in the dark on this sunless day

I yearn for release from the emptiness in me,

yearn to tell of release, of catching a new breath,

of reaching for the moon.

No one hears me.

I yearn for release – a new breath.

I have no paper, no brown bag

stuffed in a pocket…only a pen

to scribe what I see…feel.

Under the waning crescent moon of solstice

I scribe this moment on hand and sleeve

before I doze under a sliver of a silvery moon.

Awareness suddenly stirs.

The smallest of birds

sing,

calling a hint of first light

into now.

I blink. Blink again.

Questioning.

What was I thinking or needing?

Was I dreaming?

In the fading of night I see…

my need to touch, to grasp, to go home

left fingerprints on the edge of the moon.

Placeholders

this place of fear

of less than, not good enough

anchors deep within

pain by pain it builds

with more fear, more less-than

more not good enough

holding place deep within

this place of suffocation,

of nothingness,

nails shut my deep within

yet something

breathing into me says

I am better than false beliefs

carved on the heart of my soul

still, fear hovers

how do I navigate this language

being more than

being good enough, being whole

how do I breathe these into this day

and all my tomorrows

how do I brush off the residue of false beliefs

to blow away the shavings of pain

from all the heart carving

how deep do I dig to unsettle old placeholders

to forgive myself

for building this place

Star-falls

Dark sky above holds

silvery satin billowing

in the star trails,

and milky ribbons

thread themselves through the borealis.

Am I passing from darkness

into a few moments of new light?

Will I see beyond self into the self beyond?

Is the beyond, my beyond, reachable?

Loud laughing bursts from me

as I confront my audacity to question

what has been happening forever.

And I know

when the moon sees a bit less sun –

in that moment stars fall in random disorder,

scribing new directions over old horizons,

and my season of fires, challenges and doubts,

shrinks into embers.

I watch. Amazed. Exhale peacefully.

The star-falls seem so close

I stretch longer than my body

to touch just one star-fall

drifting over the waning crescent moon

just one, to hold…to flow with

what has been happening

forever

Whisper Mode

40

billion

trillion

gazillion

unlimited words

whispers from the universe

echoing possibilities

opportunities

mind is vice-tight

can't silence the in-flow

the paper, stark white,

remains blank

words trapped inside

must jump the barbed wire

must be outside

myself

40

billion

trillion

gazillion

whispers

What Is This Burden We Carry?

we carry the burden of survival

from timelines bent with tragedy

    because we rise above it

we carry the wounds

from swords, blades, and bullets

    but heal our bleeding

we carry the search for truth

in the war of words and ideologies

    so we rise above the lies

we carry the sins and histories of others

trying to reset the compass of outcomes

    but we rise above the past

we carry the task of forgiving

the sinners and haters

    for we rise above evil

we carry hearts broken, saddened

to strengthen our resolve

    and rise up to find happiness

we carry the treasure of love

because it was promised

    so we rise to pay it forward

we carry futures and possibilities

for hope is not a burden

    we rise with it

Wear gratitude like a cloak and it will feed every corner of your life.
– Rumi

Grateful

4 x 7 lines of me

I am

words I speak,

songs I sing,

inhalations, exhalations

of a million nuances

and thoughts propelling me

moment to moment

I am

my soul living this

earth plane experiment

gift of journey

incredible unexpected path

and unlimited movements

toward unknown destinations

I am

a temporary particle of dust

floating through lifetimes

coming and going

brushing by all the hopes

and dreams held in the wind

steadying my spinning compass

I am

just me, quite simple,

releasing old anchors

sailing across the world ocean

to the holy shores of divinity

and I am not afraid

of the words I speak of Love

Brought Forth

I am brought forth on the walk of Angels

travelling through the ether –

afraid to leave home yet eager to know

the place where humans *love*,

and this thing they call *love*.

Stars light a bright path aligned

with my journey into a planetary moment

in my soul's timeline.

Galaxies and star clusters brush against me

reminding me of our oneness

as the Angels and I

wait at the edge of my descent.

Angels will be my constant companion

reminding me to cherish all

as "all" is the mirror of myself,

the mirror of unconditional love within-without

reflecting the brilliance and grandeur of the sun,

while my friend Lady Moon plays the lesser role

of good humility; she also reminding me

I am one with the universe,

one with all that I see –

one with all humans,

all sentient beings, all creatures –

sharing every intricate but infinitely defined

moment of Divine breath.

From this walk with the Angels,

through the ether,

I will know humans

and human love.

My journey of good humility begins.

I am grateful.

Floating

enigma:

soul practice arrives

from the darkest part of light –

floating on fresh air into nowhere

shadow-self casts off

grace abounds

On Forgiveness

Forge ahead,

Onward.

Replay nothing.

Give thanks for

Injuries, painful moments.

Value the lessons

Even though you're

Numb.

Embrace forgiveness.

Save your own

Soul.

Prayer of Peace

May peace and harmony touch those we know,
enable kindness and compassion to circle and flow
halting the war machines of so many centuries,
replacing them with peaceful warriors and sentries.

Where love lives, the heart forgives.

May the holy energy of heaven that all should feel
fill humankind and nature with the strength of steel
to forget the atrocities made by brutal foreign forces
and release the pain imposed by war's trojan horses.

Where love lives, the heart forgives.

As suffering fades, may painful memories quickly heal
so we can feel God's hand on our soul's unsteady keel.
May our tears cleanse the wounds in our heart
so we can step forward in the light and new start.

Where love lives, the heart forgives.

Grace

What is this dream I must live,

this smack-down of take and give?

Where do I go from here,

from distances far and near?

What is between below and above?

Stop telling me it's Love!

Don't tell me there are many parallels

of me, all sifting truths from multiple hells.

Don't remind me it's this time around

I must resolve the Karma on me bound.

I must stop recycling the strident din.

No more words. No more spin.

I refuse to hear senseless talk,

refuse to crawl, amble, or walk

any further on this clichéd discourse.

So I shout out "Hear me, Source!

When will I be in the right time, right place!?"

Beloved, you're here. You never left my Grace.

I listen to my heart

Pesky, biting insect

I itch the remembrance of you.

Tiny ant crawling your existence on me

leaving a trail,

I know you deep in my core.

Thorn and thistle pricking me

until I bleed recognition

I see you wearing

the tension and liquid red of me.

Joe-Pye plume and nettle root,

make me drink your healing strength

full down to your spent leaves,

reading in you a moment of my future.

Flower, the mystery of your fragrance

imprisons me, makes me question

how from tangible beauty

the essence of you drifts unseen

lifting me beyond ego – and we are one.

Middle of the road, doe eyes –

startled, I stop and question

my path, my unstoppable speed,

my need to run the gerbil's run

without reasonable reason.

We breathe memories of our oneness.

Remind me I can let go,

I can surrender

to healing and wholeness.

Remind me, I can

embrace divinity within and without.

Remind me, we are fully one

until we are not.

Give me cause to listen to my heart.

All my pain departs in listening to my heart.

Meditation

My soul –

in sync with the fugues and vibratos of matter –

dismisses ego-self grasping at nothing

waltzing itself into a melody of emptiness

lost in breathing.

My soul –

in sync with black holes and voids

ignites with the fire-dust of the sun

settling itself into a pulsing galaxy

lost in breathing.

My soul –

in sync with the nuances of tone and tenor

crafts a journey of harmonies

honing itself into a master composition

lost in breathing.

My soul –

in sync with universal humility

drifts as a jellyfish in flow with a rhythm

gliding on a current of bliss

lost in breathing.

Rituals

4am

From shadows of worry

and the fury of Fell Beasts and dragons

riding my dreams, I awaken.

Releasing the hours of sleep

eyes rested, heart peaceful –

I feel the softness of day

awakening in the softness of itself.

I rise, breathing this new day.

Mindfully, my hands lift fresh water

to spill gracefully over face, neck, and

vessel of my soul.

Shear scarf drapes hair, shoulders,

respect and dignity touching

the universe without, universe within.

Gentle fabric flows white around me

as I stand tall before the Source of All,

the Source of me.

I wait as first light touches me.

Salutation to the Dawn

breathes easily from my voice and soul

where still it lives in Sanskrit.

Cumulus and stratus blurs

fill the fading of darkness –

soft gray mammoths and carousel animals

amble, without ambition, over a new horizon.

Waiting, hands folded, breath has depth

only this moment knows.

And I watch the shards of dawn

paint the bellies of the beasts in

broad strokes of ember red and rose-gold,

Source announcing this day *has* begun.

Joy in my heart dances with gratitude.

5am

Humbled by the gift of dawn,

I pray – *Aad Guray Nameh*,

and I bow to the Primal Wisdom.

Sometimes

Sometimes

I am lost –

I know not where I am

only

that I am deeply embedded

in that vastly tangled

barely conscious

somewhere

between mind and heart

Soul

the beauty of the soul,

this…placeholder within,

thrives in itself,

journeys,

brings itself back

to the essence of itself

as the flower returns

to its essence

before birth,

before

even

the

seed

The goal of life is to make your heartbeat match the beat of the universe, to match your nature with Nature.
– Joseph Campbell

Nature

Breaking Dawn

Cloudy monsters fade, losing their dragon-blood red
remembering only the magic and mystery
pulling the floating darkness from the dawn.

Rounded edges of misty grey cocoons shred,
the hope of rain vanishes in desert's history.
Cloudy monsters fade, losing their dragon-blood red.

Sun throws light beams from dark night's bed
across the birthing of blue into day's destiny
pulling the floating darkness from the dawn.

How vast and intense this day's dawn has bled
plunging brilliance and freshness into her chastity.
Cloudy monsters fade, losing their dragon-blood red.

This break of day clings to atoms on a thread
birds sweetly sing their serenade, their delivery
pulling the floating darkness from the dawn.

Puffy gray anacondas, open paths the sun must tread.

Red pandas drift away. No drama. No misery.

Cloudy monsters fade, losing their dragon-blood red,

pulling the floating darkness from the dawn.

Cypress in Moonlight

Italian cypress stand tall,

alert –

dark sentries

guarding the dusky skyline.

A late gentle breeze plays them.

Sentries standing tall, aroused,

waver not,

weaken not,

until…

until the breeze

carries a sweet soft breath

in the first exhalation of night.

Dark Italian sentries wait for her,

hunger for her.

Lady Moon arrives early,

touches them –

weakens them with her kiss.

They sway a bit.

Melt under her gaze.

She is pleased.

Fire Light

Edgy jagged rapiers of fire light

slamming across the surly sky left and right –

earth trembling, waiting to birth daylight.

Thundering kettle drums, pounding

on a vast graphite cloud, command attention,

and earth bowed.

Patterns

Mysterious…

the patterns

of butterfly wings

unquestionable beauty

in a thousand

colors, shapes, sizes

a divine kaleidoscope

we name "Oh, my God,

how beautiful!"

and we just know

the Infinite

simply

resides there

Winter Sky

In winter sky, clouds hold snow.

Golden autumn finds leaves that blow.

Gone the spring rains that fill the sky

and winds lifting the butterfly.

Look fast for the seasons in flow.

Summer, a gypsy all aglow,

dances on a slow hot tempo

but fire won't burn the butterfly

in winter sky.

Goodbye seedlings in embryo.

Farewell bright skies of indigo.

Adieu gold moon and leaves that die.

Cold days, cold dreams find air bone dry.

Brittle winds toss souls to-and-fro.

One cloud, two crows – a domino

in winter sky.

Simply Bold

bold yellow irises

36 in their full boldness

and carefree flutter

as if each had a young girl's

long hair tossing in the wind

8 wannabes' heads, poking at the sky,

can barely contain one more day

of their about-to-be radiance

44 lovelies gifting all of themselves

as they are, as meant to be –

no doubt, no lies, no deception, no blame

they charge up into the sun,

a simple dance of acceptance

for each bloom renewed, reglorified,

bursting into a 48-hour time capsule

holding only beginnings and endings –

no sorrow, grieving, despair,

no self-deprecation,

no need for more or less

no need to ramble, nor wallow in angst

about what is beyond them

satisfaction colors through them

to their very edges

revealing their moment of truth

in a moment of grace

Starry Night

How does the deep dark of midnight

linger so calmly, so steadily,

amid the kisses of

        a billion stars and

        a billion, trillion, gazillion or more kisses?

Is there a place in the night

untouched by these fiery kisses?

Can the far universe,

        even darker, unending,

         its "forever" unseen,

         its "beyond" unknown,

can it stay this course…

always receiving kisses,

        unending, adoring kisses,

        star upon night

        every night?

Night sky receives.

No demands, no rejections.

No grasping, no capturing,

    no clutching or taking,

    no squandering away of each fiery kiss,

    no desperation, no selfish expectancy…

        only being there,

        receiving kisses, receiving love.

Bright fiery star-lips

adoring the body of night,

giving

receiving

no demands, no expectancy

both coming together

in pleasure, and play…and love

in a timeless field of wonder.

The Sea

she

rolls in

her beauty –

dancing to shore –

calls

she

touches,

laps around

my feet, draws my

soul

she

curls fast,

her magic

pulls me into

her

i –

falling

into her

vaginal depths –

merge

Outside

Stew simmering.

Steam rising

hot, moist, burning –

lid clamps on but

steam demands

open the window!

Spring breeze, rushing in,

invites me away from

simmering steaming stew.

Outside! she pleads.

Leaves budding; birds singing;

clothes waving; trees swaying;

bees dancing; blooming scents

invading.

Stove off!

Door slams open!

Bursting out from the inside

I'm running.

Running in the *outside*

where I breathe in Oneness.

Forgive me my nonsense, as I also forgive the nonsense of those that think they talk sense.
– Robert Frost

Just for Fun

1648

'Twas Saint Mary at the Wall church

let old Humpty Dumpty slip from his perch

when Colchester fell under siege

of the Royalists and their Liege.

No more did Humpty Dumpty sit on the wall

because the enemy caused his mighty fall.

The tower blew to pieces that rambled

so Humpty Dumpty just became scrambled.

OT

I would I were an ocelot

scratch, squirm, and really grouse a lot

if my zoo scrubbed too hard each spot

for I'm too attached to the spots I've got

to be known as the sans spot ocelot

El Rey and The Homonyms

The Spanish King from his throne

was so over-thrown.

It was a terrible scene

for me to have seen.

Don't know how long he had lain

on that dirty lane.

El Rey's yelling was quite coarse,

not royal, of course.

His red face would not lessen

from this sad lesson.

"Go! Homonyms you must find!

They'll be jailed and fined!

Of this event do not write!"

"Yes, King. You're quite right."

Off I went without a cent

on the Nyms' trail, and scent.

All peasants the Nyms had won,

but not *this* sharp one.

The Nyms saw the King's bare cell,

so his lair I sell.

Then in hand, before I ate,

ten pieces of eight.

My horse and I go our way,

gold in bags to weigh.

Holiday Pie

Sing a song of sixpence, pocket full of rye;
Four and twenty blackbirds bak-ed in a pie.

The pie was heavily spiced, diced, and cleanly sliced
yet not one of twenty-four blackbirds sacrificed.

The crust split open as four and twenty flew
far from the castle to a modern home new.
Fat blackbirds now adorn my holiday tree,
I swoosh and yell but they refuse to fly free!
They're awfully noisy and very rambunctious,
and not even contrite or a bit compunctious.
Tittering and twittering and preening with play,
weighing down my holiday tree just bought today!
Fat black feathered ornaments crowd my little pine,
no space left for lights, tinsel, this garland so fine.
The biggest, and fattest, so portly and stout,
drops with its carrion on tiny top sprout,
tipping and tilting my sweet holiday tree,

now twenty-three blackbirds, a bouncing black sea.

Ignoring each other's childish petulance,

they settle again with portly arrogance.

Drama queens, each acting as Partridge in pear tree,

they cackle, caw, and sing "Look at me!… me, me, me!"

Quietly I plan, scheme and work on the sly –

big pan, big crust, and another big bird pie.

Socks

Who would ever suppose

dirty socks have a *toe-nose*?

Or a bunched-up personality

where there is no reality?

Definitely not new ones from a store.

So old ones are cast aside to the floor?

Bunched up in disregard?

Yes! Socks are just a casual discard.

But, overnight the floor holds on

until after the coming dawn

when the laundry door closes

on those silly sock noses.

Wobble-bobble

The cat's tall hat

wobbled to match ol' Tabby's tail.

Sauntering down the shady lane

Tabby didn't see that Great Dane.

His soft smooth strut dripped with ego –

he winked at friends

and himself too.

Fierce growling froze

Tabby dead still.

Bolting, he ran nearly insane

zig-zagging right down a big drain.

No more cat or hat in this tale.

Great Dane did that!

The Singing Platoon

Finding an old rune,

on the moon,

in the month of June,

with wording well hewn,

saying "Soon,

a message you will croon,

with words that impugn

a small loon

sitting on the moon."

This singing platoon,

in maroon,

jumps from a cocoon,

singing out of tune,

of a loon,

with feathers to prune.

And so, the small loon,

at high noon,

refused to commune.

Soon, the Moon Platoon,

in a swoon,

crafts a new lune tune.

"May a blue raccoon,

with bassoon,

fly high in a balloon."

But there's no raccoon,

just this lune

as a bad lampoon.

Free Range

The times were tough, and the times were leaner

for egg layin' times in COvid-nineteener.

The villagers sneaking around, lurking,

stole new borns from under the girls working.

Village children, from where all meanness hails,

piled dozens of egglets in old tin pails.

From barking dogs they ran, hiding on a side road,

hurling egglets at cars as yellow and white flowed.

Mama said "This ain't happenin' to my kid.

Don't matter the times egged on by this COvid."

Ma and her chick-friends gathered one cold night

hatching a plan in the shadows of fright,

squeezing through shredding wire to grasses greener,

desperate in times of COvid-nineteener.

They dash-darted to the fence hoping for change,

open space called them, and too… that big free range.

So Mama drops me on the other side –

far into the free range where I'm to hide.

An alarm is called out from her one brave scout,

she and chick-friends worry-scurry all about.

Farmer John was lookin' for Fox on his walk.

Each workin' girl flattened hard against a rock.

When he passed they fled across this parceled grange.

Frenzied, they scattered away from this free range.

Chick-friends all they ran lock step in a real tight group

leaving this little egglet, me, far from the coop.

I tried calling "Ma! Ma!", but Truth was silent as stone.

No squawk, no reply, and I knew I was alone.

So this was it – hiding under dung heaps thick.

Then I sprouted legs and arms thin as a stick.

A hat, eyes, mouth, cartoon hands – so very strange,

but now that I can run, they call me… Free Range.

For awhile it was fine hiding in tall grasses

until I saw sharp hooves and big bovine asses.

Dodging, darting, dropping into hardscrabble tracks,

I feared I would fall apart from too many cracks.

Seeing no future I took to the road and ran,

and what used to be greener was now big *bad* land,

hot and dusty, and no hiding place to arrange.

So I showed some swagger. Now they call me… Free Range.

I stop in towns and schools to tell my tales

of those mean children and their old tin pails,

of stick legs, and cartoon hands, darkness and fear,

being left alone, Mama shedding no tear.

The times were tough, and the times were leaner,

challenging times in COvid-nineteener –

times to be stronger, times calling for a change.

I survived alone. So, they call me… Free Range.

Those Dickens Kids

Those little kids created by Dickens

had very few if meager pickins.

And with nothing in their sacks or storage

their bowls were merely tasteless porridge.

Acknowledgments

Many thanks to the Sedona Coyote Poets for their honest feedback and encouragement. This group of brilliant poets (Ann Duchaine, Bonnie Hartenstein, Janie Rian, Kathy Mackey, Liz Hargrove, Martha Entin, Mary Scully-Whitaker, Nancy Ruby, Rose Moon, Sharron Porter, Sylvia Somerville), has brought collective energy to my creativity and writing process. They have been the best co-conspirators in the poetic arts. I am grateful for their friendship, and their constructive feedback.

My thanks go to Kate Hawkes, Producing Artistic Director of Red Earth Theatre, for giving me the opportunity to present my poetry in spoken word venues. I'm grateful also to Gary Every for featuring me and my original works in his Prose and Poetry Project. And thanks to Larry Kane for my PR portrait, and letting me use his B&W photo to accompany my poem *I Am Called*. Gratitude goes out to Paul Longstaffe and Carole Nese (facilitators of Western Edge Writers) for their feedback and time.

Of course, there's gratitude for my parents providing a college education, to my family – Bruce, Jacque, Steven, Jessie, Michael, Nicole, Molly, Tallon, Wyatt, Jon, Sam, Patrick, Lillian – and friends John Hodes, Gary Cramer, Liz Learmont, and Dee Kumar.

Thanks to Naomi C. Rose – author, editor, yoga instructor, and friend. I could not have put this book together without you.

And for my soul staying connected to this journey called Life, I give thanks. Without that there wouldn't have been any pondering on personal growth, duality, loss, love, spiritual development, life events, global events, the what ifs, and even contemplating the vastness of the universe and beyond.

I also offer deep gratitude to the Hindu deity, Sarasvati, the Hindu goddess of knowledge, music, art, speech, wisdom, and learning. Sarasvati: "she who dwells on the tongue of poets".

About the Poet

Constance Patrick obtained her B.A. Ed. from Arizona State University. She taught high school English, was right hand for the Drama department, and served as English Department Chair.

Her career shifted into business management roles, and after many years of moving around with her job, became certified in Feng Shui and spent several years teaching Feng Shui and consulting in Atlanta, Nashville, and Phoenix. She also wrote several screenplays for TV.

After moving to Sedona, AZ, Constance presented her own poetry with Sedona's Red Earth Theatre in *Kind Art from the Heart*, *Performing Stillness*, *Healing Interconnections: Nature, Spirit, Art*, *Earth Elementals*, *Gratitude Show,* and *Earth Delights,* as well as original pieces presented at the Rumi Tree Art Gallery. In recent years, she appeared in Shakespeare's Lysistrata, and was Stage Manager for Morely, and Shakespeare's Midsummer Night's Dream. Constance has also presented her original monologues with Red Earth Theatre, and the Prose and Poetry Project in Sedona.

Constance's poems have been published in *Viral Voices*, *The Stray Branch (Volumes 26 and 27)*, and *U.S. 1 Worksheets (Volumes 66 and 67)*. She also has Flash Fiction published in *The Stray Branch (Fall/Winter 2022)*. For many years Constance has developed short stories around "mountain folk" saying they are her favorite characters, and has presented some of these unique voices with Sedona's Red Earth Theatre venues.

She is a member of Sedona Coyote Poets, Western Edge Writers, and U.S.1 Worksheets Poets' Cooperative.

Creating is a remarkable journey — sometimes too big to wrap around but carving it into a Haiku, or imbedding a thimble of truth in a Rondeau or Villanelle is enough to resonate with me and others.
— CP

www.ingramcontent.com/pod-product-compliance
Lightning Source LLC
Chambersburg PA
CBHW060800050426
42449CB00008B/1462